first etude album

for violin

Compiled,
Adapted, and Edited
by HARVEY S. WHISTLER
and HERMAN A. HUMMEL

RUBANK®

HAL•LEONARD®
CORPORATION
7777 W. BLUEMOUND RD. P.O. BOX 13819 MILWAUKEE, WI 53213

1

De BERIOT

2

GEBAUER

* FR = At the frog of the bow.

3

HERMANN

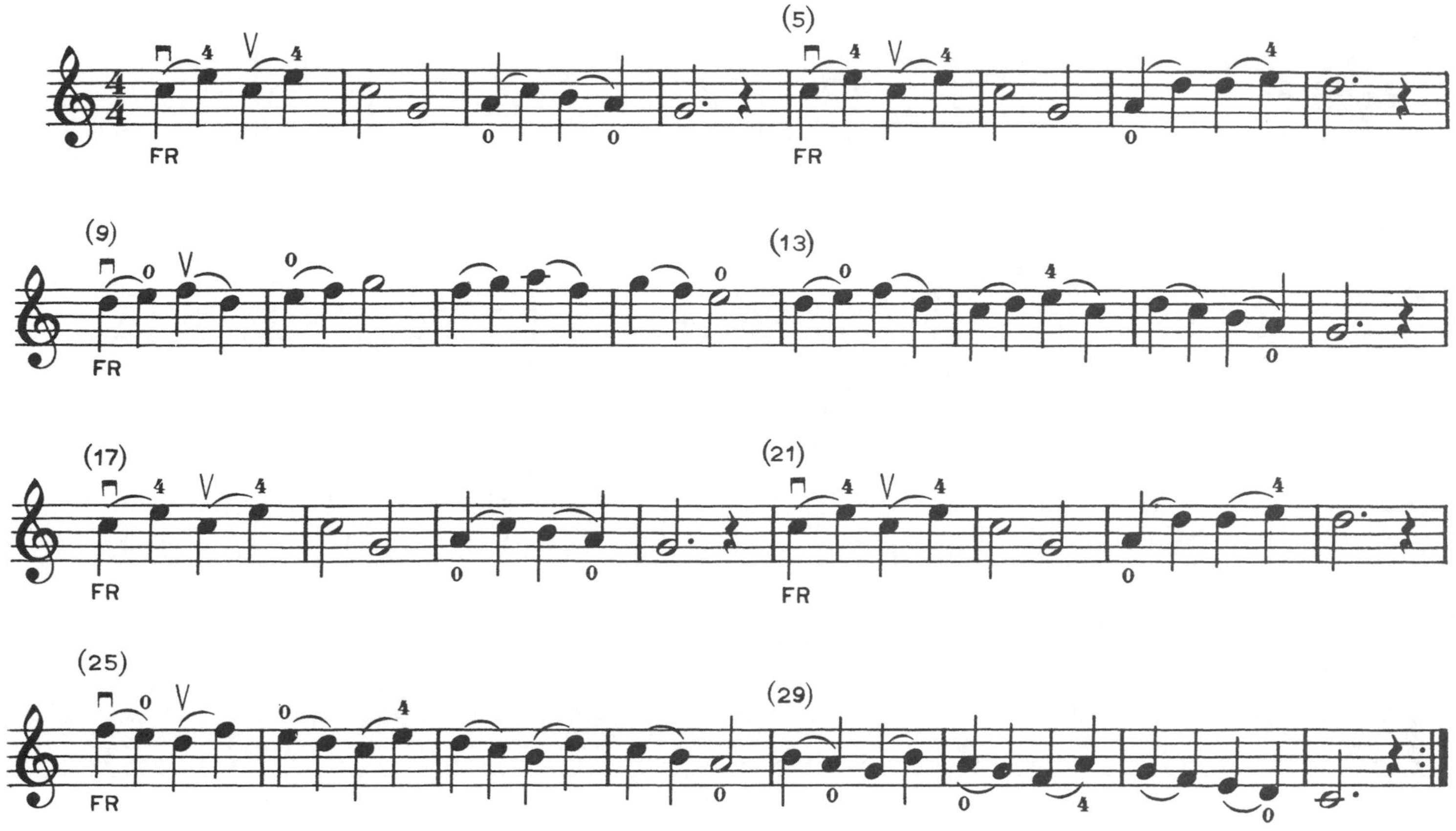

4

DANCLA

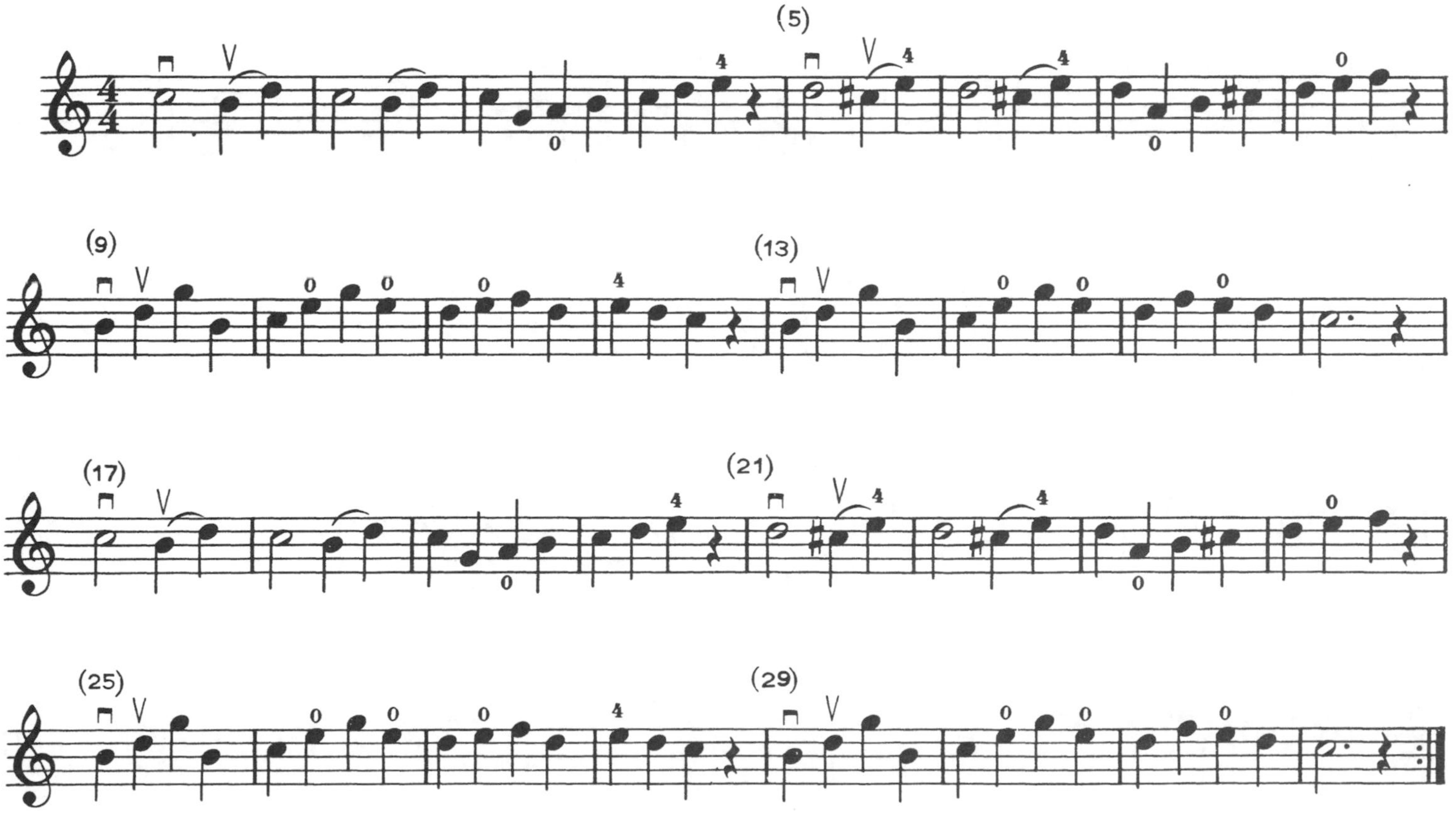

TOURS

BLUMENSTENGEL

13

TOURS

14

HOFMANN

15

HOFMANN

16

RIES

17

GRÜNWALD

18

DANCLA

21

HOFMANN

22

MAZAS

23

GRÜNWALD

24

HERMANN

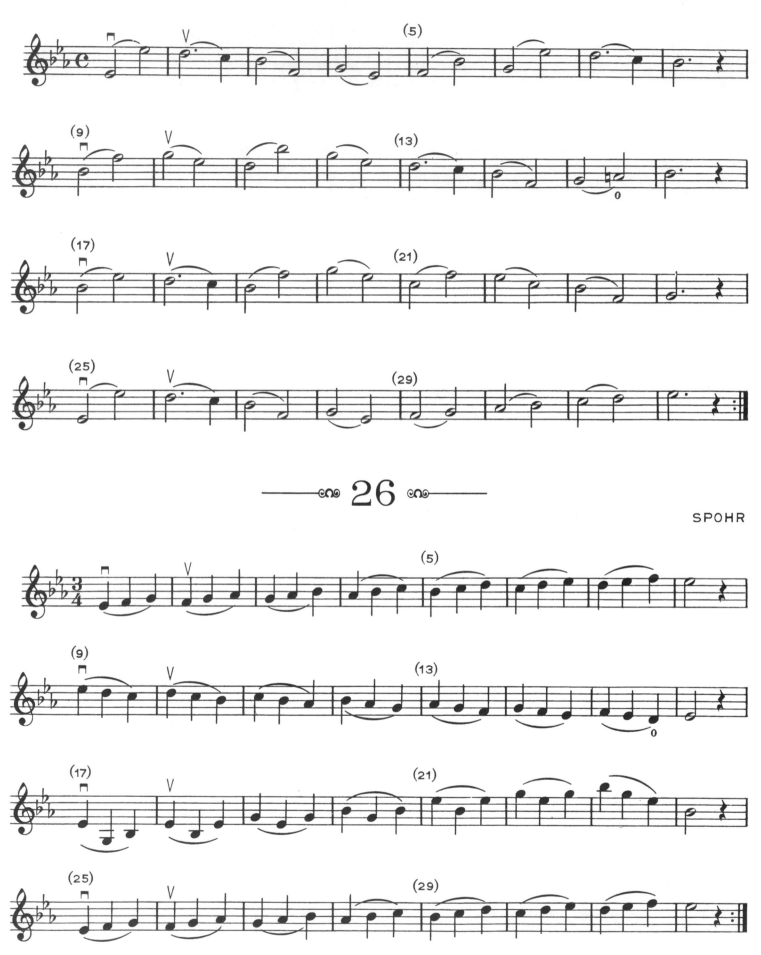

35

BÖHMER

36

SCHRADIECK

19

43

EICHBERG

44

HOFMANN

23

47

MAZAS

48

BÖHMER

49

ALARD

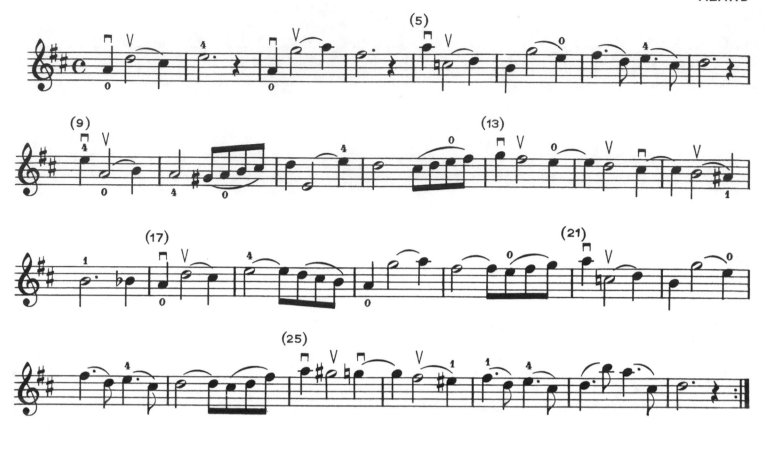

50

De BERIOT

51

ALARD

52

BÖHMER

53

SCHRADIECK

54

SCHRADIECK

55

BÖHMER

56

De BERIOT

57

HERMANN

58

DANCLA